There Was Another

A Book for Siblings After the Loss of a Twin/Multiple Baby

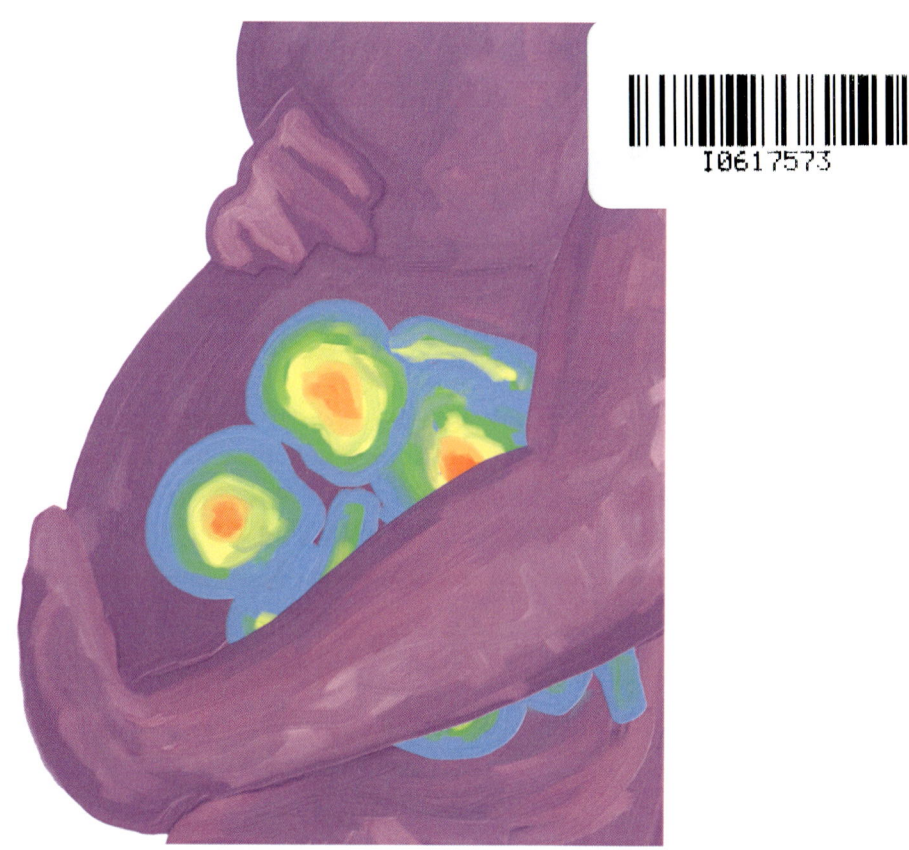

Written and Illustrated by Laura Camerona, CCLS

A
Words Worth
Repeating
Book

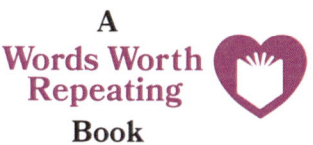

www.wordsworthrepeating.com
Des Moines, IA

Tips for Reading this Book and Supporting an Older Sibling or a Twin/Multiple as They Grow:

-A child will feel and express grief differently based on their developmental level. As they grow, children may react differently to this book and the conversations about their sibling.

- When talking about a deceased sibling, pay close attention to how this affects the living twin/multiples. As they grow, follow the living sibling's lead regarding their connection with their deceased sibling. It is natural for a child to want to feel independent and not always labeled as a "former multiple".

-Be mindful about memorials on birthdays. In most situations, it makes sense to spend the birthday celebrating the living child(ren), and consider picking a different date for a memorial.

-Follow the child's lead. If your child isn't in the mood to read the book, save it for another moment.

- Stop and answer questions. If in the middle of the book your child wants to talk about one part of the book or one question that they have, set the book aside and focus on that.

- Bedtime often isn't the best time for books about topics that kids may have questions or big feelings about. It might lead to trouble sleeping. Try to avoid reading this book right before bedtime.

-Don't expect a certain outward reaction from your child. It is okay if your child doesn't show the emotions that you might expect.

-If your child asks questions or reacts in a way that you don't feel comfortable with, contact a local mental health professional.

Dedicated to all of the babies who made an impact on this world, no matter how long they spent in it.

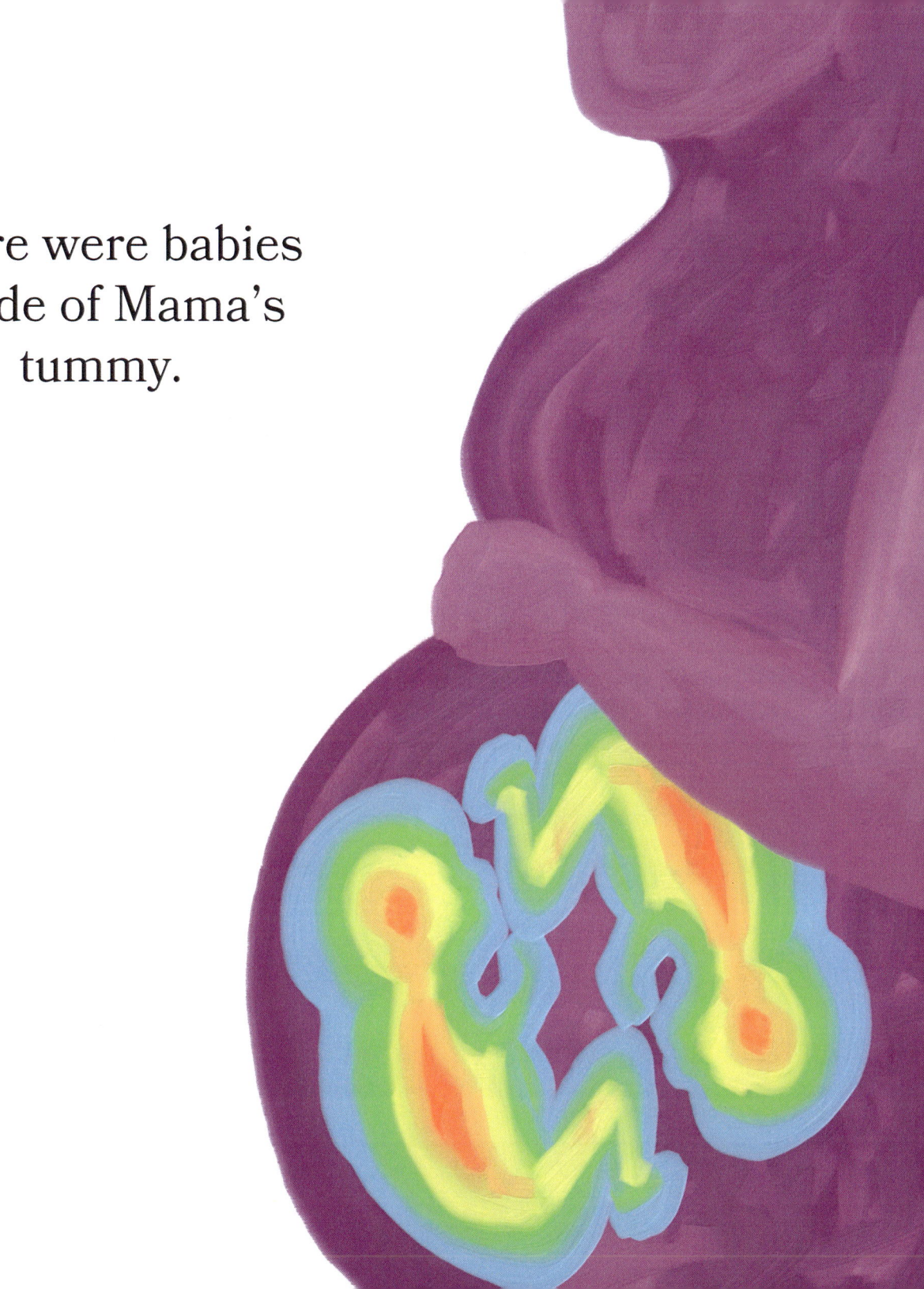

There were babies
inside of Mama's
tummy.

Our whole family would rub Mama's belly and talk to the babies.

The babies
were warm
and cozy
inside.

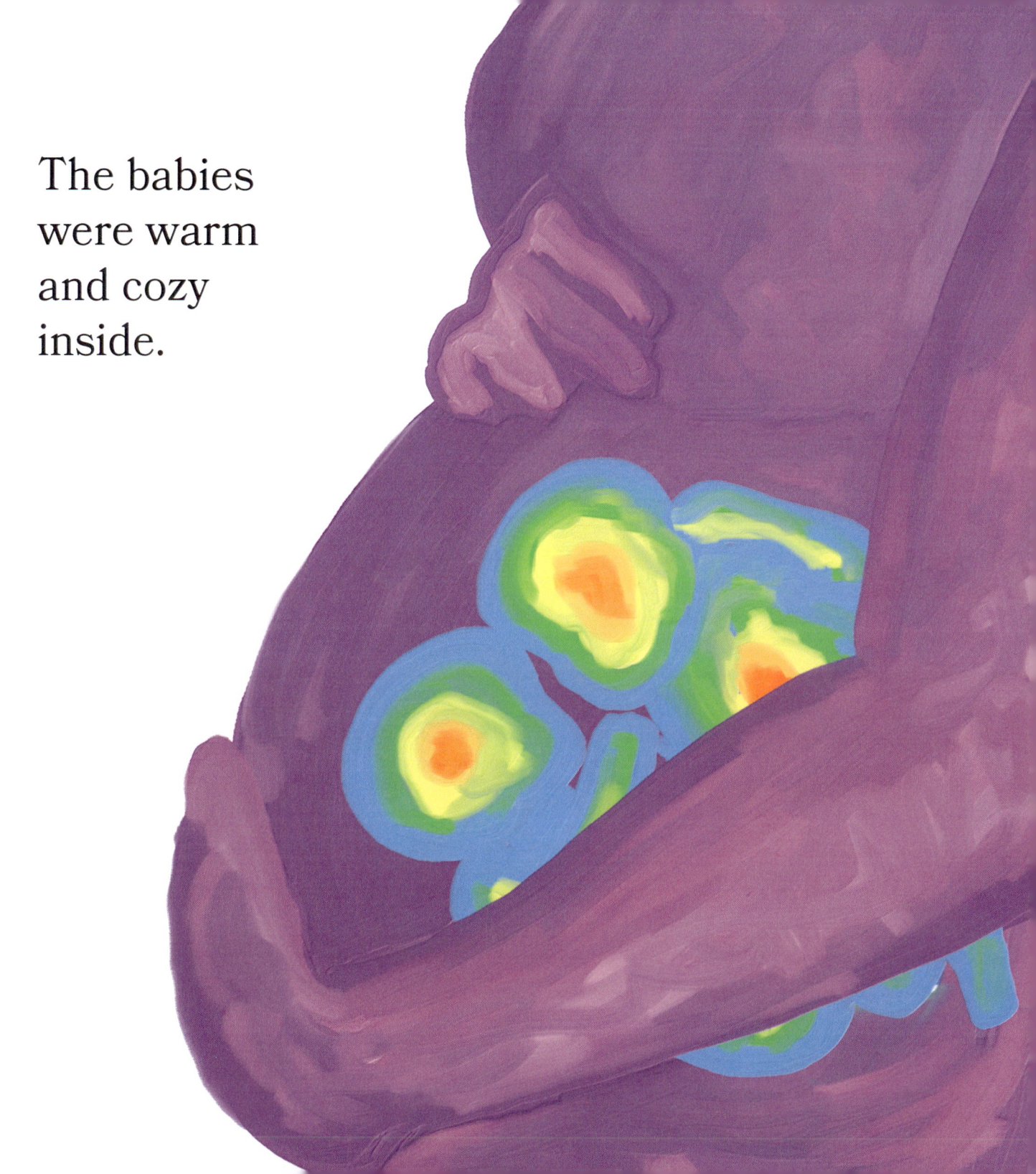

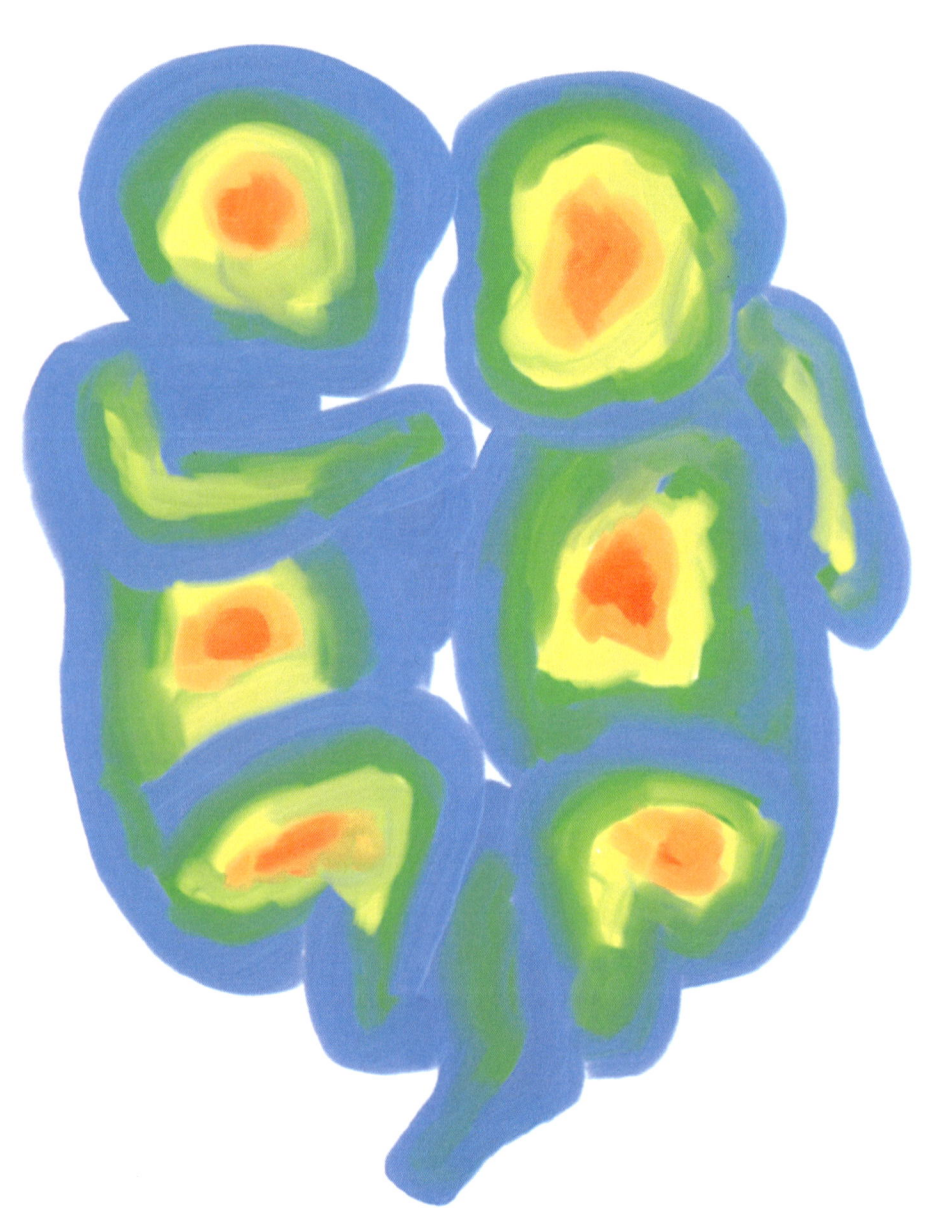

When they were growing in Mama, the babies would snuggle and hold hands.

The babies grew bigger and bigger, right next to each other.

Our whole family dreamed of what the babies would be like. Our family dreamed about who they would grow to be.

Lots of babies grow in tummies and
come out when they are big and healthy.

Our baby didn't grow
this way.

Something very sad
happened.

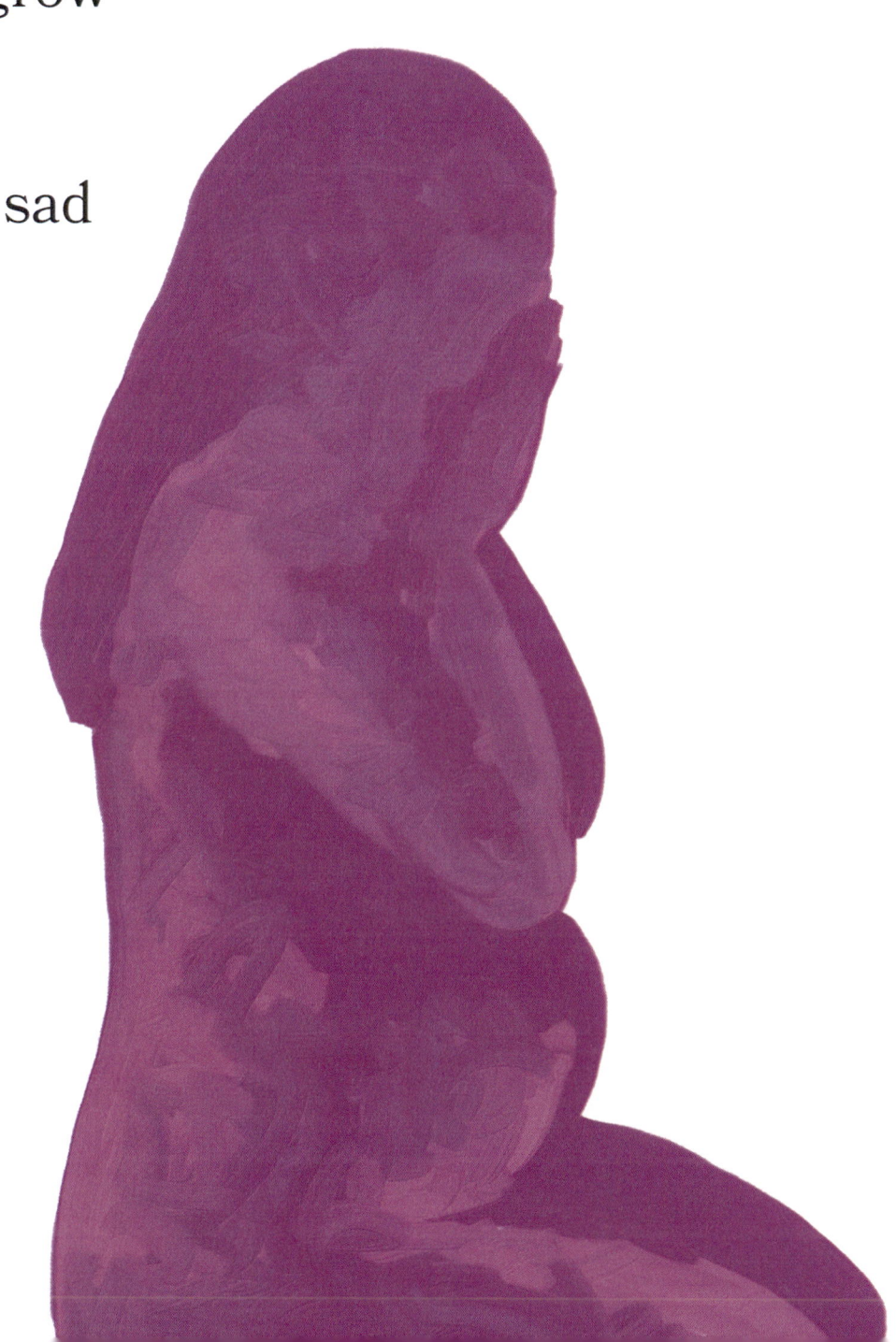

One of our
babies died.

Doctors wanted to help.
Sometimes, there are things
that doctors can't fix.

We don't know why this happened
to one of our babies. It's no one's fault.
Sometimes, sad things happen.

My family is sad. We all wish that our baby could be alive and healthy. We all wish that all of our babies would come home to live with us.

Our family has so much love for our baby that died.

Of course, my family has so much
love for all of our babies.
Every child in our family is so special.

Some days when my family feels sad,
I feel sad too. Some days when my family is
sad, I feel happy.

It's okay to feel how I feel.

We aren't the only family that this has happened to. When babies grow inside tummies, this happens sometimes.

Even though our baby died,
I am still their sister or brother.

That will never change.

Our baby who died reminds my family how strong our love is.

Our
baby
felt
our
love.

Sometimes, I think about our baby.
I think about what it would have been like
if the baby was still alive.

My family still thinks about
this baby too.

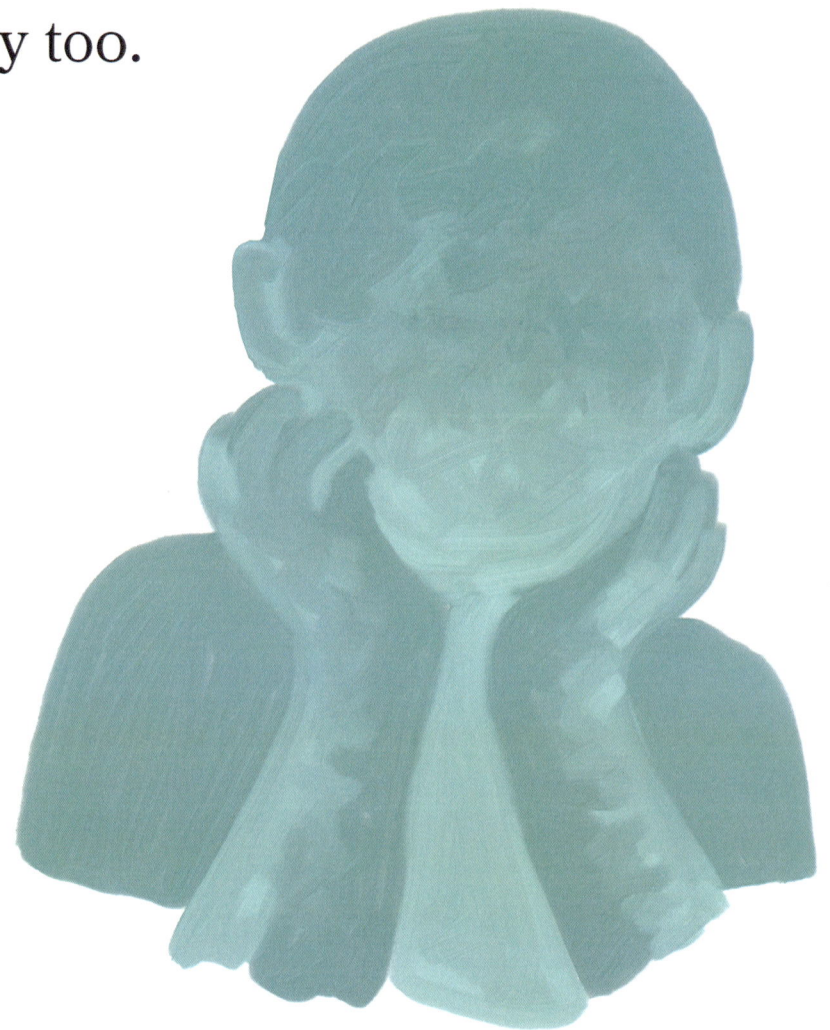

Some of us think about the baby a lot.
Some of us think about the baby
every once in while.

No matter what,
we will be connected to
our baby forever.

We will always remember
that there was another.

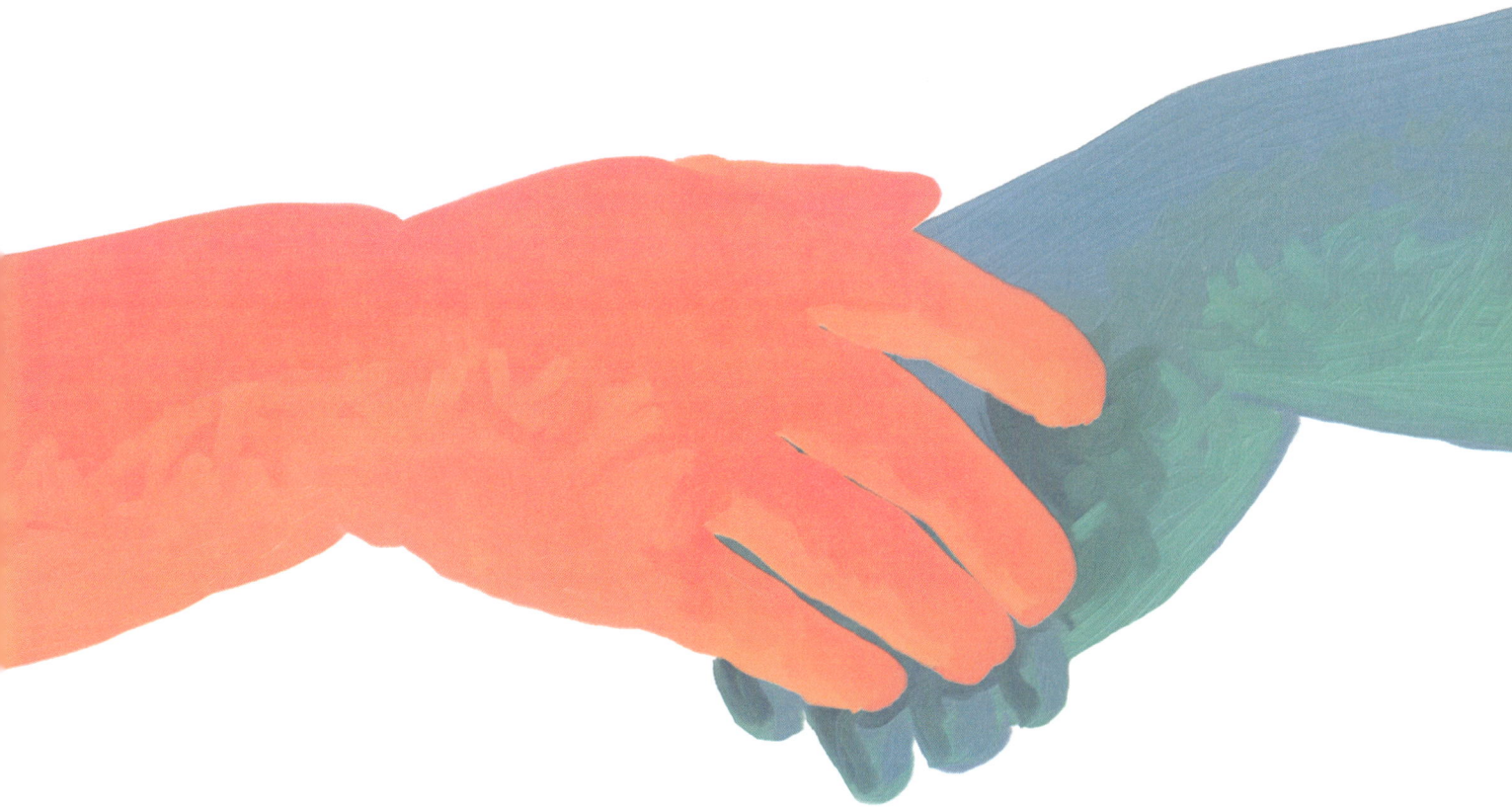

We can come up
with ways to
remember our
baby. Our
family can talk
about our baby.
We could make
a special piece
of artwork that
reminds us of
our baby, or we
can pick
certain days to
light a special
candle or visit a
special place.

There was another baby, and
that baby will always be a part of our family.

Special Projects Families Can Create Together

Some families have the opportunity to get their baby's hand prints or foot prints. Even if you have only one set of actual prints, you can use a scanner or an app on your phone to make more copies. Here are some examples of things you can create with these prints.

💛 **Family Tree:** Create a family tree and use every person in the family's prints (hand or foot) as the leaves of a tree. This can be done on a canvas or digitally.

💛 **Butterflies:** Have your child create a footprint butterfly and make one with the baby's footprints on the same canvas or paper.

💛 **Frame Art:** Buy or repurpose a frame with wide and flat sides. Have your child decorate the frame however they wish. Display the baby's prints in this frame.

Some families like to create a special place in their home or yard to remember their baby. Children can help create artwork that is displayed in this area. Here are some art projects that they can create.

💛 **Candle:** Start with a clear glass or jar. Have your child cut or tear tissue paper shapes. If they are older, they could cut it into hearts or the baby's name. Then have your child glue them to the outside of the glass with Mod Podge or a school glue and water mixture (1 cup glue to 1/3 cup water). Have them coat the entire outside of the glass with the Mod Podge/glue mixture and add jewels if you desire. After the project dries, insert a candle into the glass. Find times as a family to light the candle and think or talk about your baby.

💛 **Garden Stone:** Purchase a Garden Stone kit at your local craft store. Have your child help decorate the stone and if you wish, add your baby's name to it. Place it in your yard or garden where you can visit it.

💛 **Tree/Flower:** As a family, plant a flower or tree in memory of your baby.

Special Projects Families Can Create Together (continued)

Some families like to create something that they can wear or keep close on some days. Here are some ideas of things that children can help make.

 Family Necklace/Bracelet: Provide your child a variety of beads (most craft stores have a "mix pack") and a string. Have your child choose a bead for each family member. The bead could be symbolic based on color, shape, anything! If they don't do it on their own, ask if they would like to include a bead for the baby. If they chose not to, that is okay. You can talk about what a great team your family is during this project and how strong your love is.

 Paper Beads: Better activity for older children. Provide scrapbook paper. Have the child chose paper that is special to them. Have them cut a long thin triange (approximately 3/4 in wide and 9 in long). On the white side, have them write a message to themselves, the baby's name, anything! Starting on the wide end wind the paper tightly, so that the message on the inside of the bead and the colorful side is out. Rolling it with a pencil or straw can be helpful. Seal with Mod Podge or school glue/water mix (1 cup glue/1/3 cup water).

Some families like to create something that they won't see every day, but that they will see every so often or on special holidays to remember their baby. Here are some ideas of things that kids can help create.

 Holiday Ornament: Find a simple flat ornament or a ball and add the baby's name to it. Allow your child to decorate.

 Blank Book/ScrapBook: Use a blank book or journal and fill the pages with family memories of being pregnant, photos, pictures your child draws, write out feelings everyone is feeling, anything. Get the book out on days when your family wants to spend more time remembering your baby.

Laura Camerona, Certified Child Life Specialist

After 15 years of working in a hospital, Laura started creating books to help families and promote healing, as they continue their journey outside of the hospital.

Laura is now especially focused on helping families have hard conversations and get through challenging times together. As a Mom of three, she promotes giving kids honest, gentle, and developmentally-appropriate explanations. She believes in family resiliency and believes that families develop the best coping when they go through things together.

To learn more about Laura's other resources and services, go to www.wordsworthrepeating.com

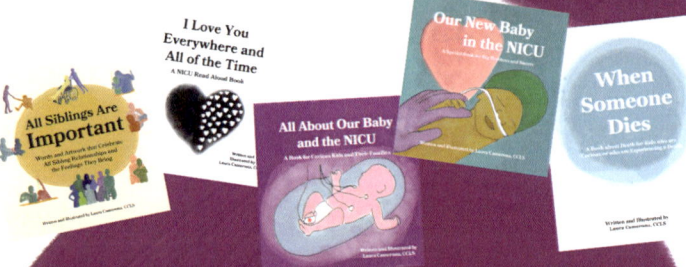

Words Worth Repeating creates books that promote positive coping and healing for kids and families. There are WWR books about a variety of topics. They can be found on the WWR website. Above are a few books appropriate for siblings during a NICU stay or after a death.

Words Worth Repeating also creates customized Journey Books for families who can't find the "right book" about a new diagnosis or stressful event. Families work directly with a Child Life Specialist to create these customized books that give words for hard situations. Contact us to learn more!

Words Worth Repeating
www.wordsworthrepeating.com